GRACE

GRACE

>> **MORE THAN WE DESERVE, GREATER THAN WE IMAGINE**

MAX LUCADO

A PARTICIPANT'S GUIDE TO SMALL GROUP STUDY

WRITTEN BY AMANDA HALEY

THOMAS NELSON
Since 1798

NASHVILLE   DALLAS   MEXICO CITY   RIO DE JANEIRO

Published in Nashville, Tennessee, by Thomas Nelson. Thomas Nelson is a registered trademark of Thomas Nelson, Inc.

Thomas Nelson, Inc., titles may be purchased in bulk for educational, business, fund-raising, or sales promotional use. For information, please e-mail SpecialMarkets@ ThomasNelson.com.

Unless otherwise noted, Scripture quotations are taken from The New King James Version®. © 1982 by Thomas Nelson, Inc. Used by permission. All rights reserved.

Scripture quotations marked NASB are from The New American Standard Bible®. © The Lockman Foundation 1960, 1962, 1963, 1968, 1971, 1972, 1973, 1975, 1977, 1995. Used by permission.

Scripture quotations marked NIV are from The Holy Bible, New International Version®, NIV®. © 1973, 1978, 1984 by Biblica Inc.™ Used by permission of Zondervan. All rights reserved worldwide.

Scripture quotations marked NLT are from The Holy Bible, New Living Translation. © 1996. Used by permission of Tyndale House Publishers, Inc., Wheaton, Illinois 60189. All rights reserved.

ISBN: 978-1-4016-7584-4

Printed in the United States of America

16 RRD 10

. . . for all have sinned and fall short of the glory of God, being justified freely by His grace through the redemption that is in Christ Jesus.

Romans 3:23–24

B. Pendleton

CONTENTS

God's grace has
a drenching about it.
A wildness about it.
A white-water, riptide,
turn-you-upside-
downness about it.
Grace comes after you.

INTRODUCTION

In a world of checks and balances, works and rewards, judgments and penalties, *grace* is a difficult concept. We can't reconcile it. We can't earn it. We don't have to pay it back. And, like most of humanity, we'll never completely understand it. But we can accept grace and give it to others.

We know *grace* as a noun, but Max tells us to think of *grace* as a verb. It is an action. It's not enough to read about grace; we must experience it. It is only because God graced us with the sacrifice of his Son that we can grace others with kindness, forgiveness, understanding, mercy, favor, and most importantly knowledge of God's grace. Therefore, understanding grace begins with accepting God's grace and practicing it in our everyday lives. Why not begin with those closest to us?

Grace is the voice
that calls us to change
and then gives us the
power to pull it off.

WHY STUDY
WITH A SMALL GROUP?

A relationship with God is personal; the grace he has given each of us is unique because each individual is uniquely made. Our experiences and our errors differ. Our paths to knowing God vary from person to person. Still, God's grace in our lives should be apparent to the world. Remember the children's song "This Little Light of Mine"? It encourages both the singers and the listeners to keep the fire of God's grace burning in their own hearts and to expose that fire to the world. Jesus showed us how to do both: He prayed silently with his Father (Luke 6:12). He preached to large crowds (Matthew 11:7) and developed close relationships with a small group of disciples (Mark 3:14). His actions were then modeled by the first-century church, who were encouraged to pray diligently (Ephesians 6:18) and then meet as groups to read the words of the apostles (Colossians 4:16) and live every aspect of life together in their small communities (Acts 2:44).

How does this model of personal relationship with God and public interaction with others fit into our technologically connected but relationship-challenged world? It's easy to pray and study by ourselves, even easier to pull up a preacher's sermon on our laptops. Maybe it's a little harder to get up from our desk chairs and drive across town to study with other Christians, but the effort has value. If prayer were enough to experience God, then Jesus would have spent three years on his knees instead of speaking from hilltops. If listening to a Sunday sermon were enough for personal growth, then he would have spent every minute preaching to thousands instead of gracing his "small group" of disciples with his love and knowledge.

Consider the dynamics within that small group of men. These men traveled to the same cities, ate the same foods, and slept in the same places. Every morning Jesus woke up surrounded by twelve smelly, often-grumbling men. Why would the God-man put himself through this? Jesus knew that relationships are best developed within a small group and that those relationships then develop us as individuals, so he graced us with his earthly presence. Those you are around most frequently are the most likely to hold you accountable. They know your worst parts and your best parts, and they aren't afraid to address the former and praise the latter. Just ask the apostle Peter (Matthew 16:16–19, 22–23).

HOW TO STUDY
WITH A SMALL GROUP

Like a close-knit family, each member of a small group should strive to know the others well. Within the group, during meetings secrets may be revealed, successes celebrated, beliefs argued, and losses grieved. In such an emotionally charged environment, it is helpful to remember a few guidelines. In fact, you may find them useful for all of your social interactions.

1. COMMITMENT

At your first meeting, the leader will give you a worksheet entitled "Grace Goals." This sheet will detail your personal goals for this study and the group's objectives. Individual commitment to the group raises the importance of the study and recognizes the value of each member. The group should agree on and commit to items such as meeting time, meeting structure, child care, study goals, homework expectations, and the number of participants.

2. CONSIDERATION

Courtesy and mutual respect lay a foundation for a thriving group. Balanced conversations lead to balanced relationships. Ensure that everyone has a chance to speak. The more you share, the more others will learn about you. The more you listen, the more you learn about others.

If you disagree with someone in the group, remember that healthy discussions are the goal. The small group should be a safe place for all members, even those whom you think are wrong. Be sensitive to others' perspectives, and show them the grace you would like to receive should you say something controversial.

3. CONFIDENTIALITY

As the study progresses, you will be encouraged to share your stories of grace you've received and grace you've given. If a story is sensitive in nature, respect the confidentiality of the person who is sharing. Don't let your conversations leave the small group.

4. COUNSEL

Just as your small group is not a place to spread gossip, it is also not a place to force your opinions, to tell others "what you should have done." Commit to listening to one another, but refrain from offering unsolicited advice.

5. CREED

It's worth emphasizing. As you study and discuss *grace* the noun, remember to practice *grace* the verb. Treat each other with the amazing, unending grace Jesus gave you when he was on the cross. Grace was given to all of us at Calvary, and you can give and receive it again within your small group. So make the motto of your group "GRACE HAPPENS HERE."

HOW TO USE THIS GUIDE

Before every small group session, you will have some homework to complete. You might argue, "But I haven't done homework in years! I don't have time to add anything else to my already-packed schedule." Everyone in your group will understand that sentiment because time is tight for all of us. But if you have joined a small group, then you have pledged to invest your life and your time in other people. Make the most of this opportunity by being prepared. Take sufficient time throughout the week to read each session's corresponding chapters in the book, *Grace*, and to answer the questions in this study guide.

When you meet with your small group, each session will begin with a short DVD presentation of the main ideas about *grace* from that week's homework. Then your leader will start a discussion based on the study questions you've considered and answered throughout the week. During the time you meet, the group might not make it all the way through the questions. Some might be more poignant to you than others; some might spark conversations that seem off-topic. That's okay. Let the Holy Spirit move through your conversations and bind you together as group members. And always remember that during your small group time, GRACE HAPPENS HERE.

When grace
happens, we receive
not a nice compliment
from God but a new
heart. Give your heart
to Christ, and he
returns the favor.

THE GRACE-SHAPED LIFE

Study Grace

Read chapter 1 from *Grace* before beginning your study this week.

Grace isn't just a noun. Yes, God gives us grace, but then he uses that very grace to change us. We become more like him, able to gracefully bestow grace on others. No one illustrates the life-changing power of grace better than the apostle Paul, the Christian hater–turned–Christ lover.

Prior to Paul's Christian ministry, which Max references in the session 1 video, the apostle learned a great deal about grace. Before his name was changed to "Paul," Saul was a highly educated Jew intent on stamping out the growing community of Jews who recognized Jesus as the Christ, their Savior. After presiding over Stephen's capital punishment in Jerusalem (Acts 8:1), Saul traveled to Damascus to deliver the high priest's arrest warrants for Jesus followers living there.

As he journeyed he came near Damascus, and suddenly a light shone around him from heaven. Then he fell to the ground, and heard a voice saying to him, "Saul, Saul, why are you persecuting Me?"

And he said, "Who are You, Lord?"

Then the Lord said, "I am Jesus, whom you are persecuting. It is hard for you to kick against the goads."

So he, trembling and astonished, said, "Lord, what do You want me to do?"

Then the Lord said to him, "Arise and go into the city, and you will be told what you must do."

And the men who journeyed with him stood speechless, hearing a voice but seeing no one. Then Saul arose from the ground, and when his eyes were opened he saw no one. But they led him by the hand and brought him into Damascus. And he was three days without sight, and neither ate nor drank. (Acts 9:3–9)

This experience may not have seemed much like grace at first. But that quick encounter with the Lord, though it left him disabled, made Saul long for more of Jesus in his life. By the time Ananias arrived to deliver God's grace to Saul and restore his eyesight, Saul was literally hungry for grace, thirsty for grace. In fact, Saul was so full of grace that it bubbled up in his heart and spilled out of his mouth: "Immediately he preached the Christ in the synagogues, that He is the Son of God" (Acts 9:20).

> Think back to a time when you realized you were wrong. How did you respond? Did you try to justify your behavior, or did you speak the truth?

> Are you always ready to proclaim God's grace, no matter where you are or who your audience is? Why or why not?

Thankfully God doesn't always allow such suffering before he exercises his grace. Long before Saul met Jesus, God had blessed Saul with the intelligence and desire to absorb God's laws into his very being. But as a well-educated Pharisee (Acts 23:6), Saul had developed his own interpretations of the Scriptures, and his stubborn, know-it-all tendencies were allowing incorrect doctrine to separate him from God's grace. Knowledge of God kept him from knowing God. That's why Jesus arrived with grace to reveal Saul's errors and to humble him. After Saul "thought about what he'd done" for three days, he was ready to receive the graceful gift of Jesus' heart into his body.

> God knew Saul needed to hit rock bottom before he would be willing to let go of his own interpretations of the law and recognize and absorb God's grace. When has stubbornness kept you from enjoying all the benefits of grace?

> God gives you grace every day. Think of something that happened today that was evidence of God's grace in your life. Did you thank him for it? Did you realize it was him at the time?

> How can you raise your awareness of God's daily grace in your life?

> Have you ever been aware of God using you as a vessel for his grace as he did Ananias (Acts 9:10–17)? Did you cheerfully embark on his mission, or did you allow your own fear or stubbornness to delay his plans?

> What are some ways you can be a vessel of grace to

• your coworkers,

• your family members,

- or your neighbors?

After accepting God's grace and letting it change him, Saul changed his name to Paul and started preaching and writing about God's grace. God's grace informed the rest of Paul's life on earth, and we are blessed to have access to some of his sermons and writings in the New Testament. Let's take a look at a few of Paul's messages that Max references in *Grace* and the session 1 video.

In a letter to his young apostle, Titus, Paul mentioned the centrality of grace in the organization and development of the church and its members:

> For the grace of God that brings salvation has appeared to all men, teaching us that, denying ungodliness and worldly lusts, we should live soberly, righteously, and godly in the present age, looking for the blessed hope and glorious appearing of our great God and Savior Jesus Christ, who gave Himself for us, that He might redeem us from every lawless deed and purify for Himself His own special people, zealous for good works. (Titus 2:11–14)

> What did Paul tell Titus that grace brings to us?

> What does grace teach us to change in our lives?

> What does grace look forward to?

> How does grace change our actions once it gives us new hearts?

As Max points out, we are clearly missing the magnitude of God's grace in our lives if we only see it as something we receive. Remember that grace is an action, and we must enact grace in order to experience it properly. Imagine if Paul had just accepted God's grace and never put it into action. If so, the gospel of grace might not have reached beyond the Jews to the Gentiles such as those living in Crete and Colossae and Galatia.

Paul described to the Gentiles his understanding of the "mystery" of Christ working in us:

> . . . the word of God, the mystery which has been hidden from ages and from generations, but now has been revealed to His saints. To them God willed to make known what are the riches of the glory of this mystery among the Gentiles: which is Christ in you, the hope of glory. Him we preach, warning every man and teaching every man in all wisdom, that we may present every man perfect in Christ Jesus. (Colossians 1:25–28)

> What is the great "mystery" that has now been revealed to the church?

> How is "Christ in you" a description of grace?

> What is required for us to "present every man perfect in Christ Jesus"?

When writing to the Jesus followers in Galatia, Paul told the story of an encounter he had with Peter. Soon after the Holy Spirit came upon him, Peter had a vision explaining that no foods were unclean—the law was obsolete in light of Jesus' death on the cross (Acts 10:9–16). But a few years later, when confronted with Jews who still ate only kosher meals, Peter returned to his own kosher roots. Paul chastised him for this weakness of faith, as he quoted here for the Galatians to read:

> For I through the law died to the law that I might live to God. I have been crucified with Christ; it is no longer I who live, but Christ lives in me; and the life which I now live in the flesh I live by faith in the Son of God, who loved me and gave Himself for me. I do not set aside the grace of God; for if righteousness comes through the law, then Christ died in vain. (Galatians 2:19–21)

As he explained to Peter and the Galatians, Paul understood that once we accept grace, once "Christ lives in" us, there is no longer a need for the law. It cannot save us, and we don't need it to guide our actions once we only act in grace.

> How was Paul "crucified with Christ"? How can we claim that too?

> We do not follow the Mosaic law as Peter and Paul once did. Instead, what things bind us and direct our actions? What must we "die to" in order to "live to God"?

> How do "faith in the Son of God" and "Christ [living] in [you and] me" work together?

Discuss Grace

At the beginning of the session with your small group, watch Max's video that accompanies this Bible study. Take some time to discuss what you and your group members learned from chapter 1 in *Grace*, your personal studies of this week's lesson, and Max's message. Then consider these questions as a small group:

> Has God performed a heart transplant in you?

> What motivations are in your heart that shouldn't be there?

> What will it take for you to be like Paul, to have a heart that beats only for Jesus?

> With your small group, decide on an activity you can complete together in the next month that will reveal grace to someone in your community. Here are a few ideas to start your conversation:

- Commit to giving time on a Saturday helping to build a Habitat for Humanity house in your community.

- Go to the Red Cross and give blood or platelets.

- Adopt a poor family in your community during the Christmas season.

- Volunteer regularly at a food bank.

- Host a "Parents' Night Out" at your church, and babysit young couples' children for free.

- Do some repair work at the home of an elderly citizen or single parent.

Conclusion / Prayer

Close your group time by taking prayer requests and praying for one another.

Notes

JESUS
STOOPED **LOW**
TO TAKE **OUR** PLACE

Study Grace

Read chapter 2 from *Grace* before beginning your study this week.

In the last session, Max reminded us that grace is an action. It is something Jesus gave to us when he died on the cross and something we give to others when we practice grace for their benefit. Just as we can continually show grace to others through our actions, Jesus is continually showing grace to us. He is in heaven, right now, arguing on our behalf to God the Father for him to forgive our sins.

Jesus has always been in the business of helping sinners. We may not be able to see him in the flesh now, but we can read about how he practiced grace on earth thanks to the record of the apostle John. In the session 2 video, Max retells John's story of how Jesus treated an adulterous woman:

> Now early in the morning He came again into the temple, and all the people came to Him; and He sat down and taught them.

33

Then the scribes and Pharisees brought to Him a woman caught in adultery. And when they had set her in the midst, they said to Him, "Teacher, this woman was caught in adultery, in the very act. Now Moses, in the law, commanded us that such should be stoned. But what do You say?" This they said, testing Him, that they might have something of which to accuse Him. But Jesus stooped down and wrote on the ground with His finger, as though He did not hear. (John 8:2–6)

Jesus bent down to the ground, made himself lower than all of his students, lower than the accusers, lower than even the woman being accused. This is a picture of his grace in action. Jesus, for the rest of his life, would stoop down so that we could be raised up. He would stoop to wash the disciples' feet, to carry his cross, and to walk out of his grave.

> What do we learn from watching Jesus, the God of the Universe, humble himself and bend down to offer grace to sinners?

No one is Too BAD to be SAVED

> Are we willing to humble ourselves to show grace to fellow sinners and less-fortunate people around us?

Jesus' demonstration of humility resulted in the humbling of the accusers and the rescue of the woman. Humility was, in this case, the catalyst for grace.

> So when they continued asking Him, He raised Himself up and said to them, "He who is without sin among you, let him throw a stone at her first." And again He stooped down and wrote on the ground. Then those who heard it, being convicted by their conscience, went out one by one, beginning with the oldest even to the last. And Jesus was left alone, and the woman standing in the midst. When Jesus had raised Himself up and saw no one but the woman, He said to her, "Woman, where are those accusers of yours? Has no one condemned you?"
>
> She said, "No one, Lord."
>
> And Jesus said to her, "Neither do I condemn you; go and sin no more." (John 8:7–11)

What about those accusers? They were taking God's law, which was intended to bring his people closer to him, and using it to separate sinners from God. At first glance, the accusers were using God's law to test a sinner. But look deeper. The accusers' true intention was to manipulate the law to test God himself, incarnate in Jesus.

In the book of Revelation, John described another Accuser, one who acted a lot like these men. John was having a vision of heaven, and he heard a voice say, "For the Accuser has been thrown down to earth—the one who accused our brothers and sisters before our God day and night" (Revelation 12:9–10 NLT). Satan is that great Accuser.

> Satan used those men to strike the woman with guilt, to test the limits of Jesus' grace. Who or what has Satan used to assault you with guilt?

> What must you do to avoid Satan's guilt trips?

Thankfully, Jesus doesn't leave us defenseless against this Accuser. He doesn't just stoop to save us, but he stands to save us. Jesus is our Advocate: "And if anyone sins, we have an Advocate with the Father, Jesus Christ the righteous" (1 John 2:1). Jesus is in heaven right now arguing on our behalf before God. He's better than any lawyer you could hire because he is always there, and he always wins. The writer of the letter to the Hebrews agreed with John that "He is also able to save to the uttermost those who come to God through Him, since He always lives to make intercession for them" (Hebrews 7:25).

> How does Jesus "make intercession" for us?

> Have you ever had the opportunity to stand up for someone
> else? How did that person react when you graced him or her
> with your support?

> Has anyone ever stood up on your behalf and advocated for you? How was this a picture of Jesus' perpetual gift of grace?

Discuss Grace

At the beginning of the session with your small group, watch Max's video that accompanies this Bible study. Take some time to discuss what you and your group members learned from chapter 2 in *Grace*, your personal studies of this week's lesson, and Max's message. Then consider these questions as a small group:

> Think of a time when Jesus "stooped" or "stood" to save you from your sin. How did his grace differ from the world's judgment?

> What things do you find Satan consistently accusing you of doing wrong, maybe even after you've repented? What can you do to shift your focus from the guilt he causes to the grace Jesus offers?

> When you see others struggling with the memory of past sins, what can you say or do to remind them that Jesus, who has removed their guilt, is their Advocate in heaven?

Conclusion / Prayer

Close your group time by taking prayer requests and praying for one another.

Notes

YOU CAN REST NOW

Study Grace

Read chapter 4 from *Grace* before beginning your study this week.

From the moment we are born, we learn that hard work yields results. Want to walk across the room without falling? Keep trying. Want to win the championship? Keep practicing. Babies learn to walk. Athletes win trophies. Executives earn bonuses. The world is a results-oriented place, where only tangible successes count.

Max tells us that, when he was in middle school, he loved this system. He liked knowing where he stood in the world, knowing that he was a success because of the number of merit badges on his Boy Scout sash. *But when it comes to salvation*, he wondered, *what tangible proof is there? Can I ever do enough? Will I ever be good enough?* No. None of us can ever do or be enough to earn heaven.

That's why God invented *grace*. When God sent his Son to earth to be crucified, he paid all the debts we'll ever owe by making the only sacrifice we'll ever need for our sins; he earned our salvation for us. Then he gave it to us. That's grace. As Paul said, "For by grace you have been saved through faith, and that not of yourselves; it is the gift of God, not of works, lest anyone should boast" (Ephesians 2:8–9). We can't earn it because Jesus has already done all the work. All we can do is accept it by having faith that Jesus' death was enough to save us.

> In his letter to the Ephesians, Paul was writing to first-century Jewish and Gentile Christians who were arguing over whether or not it is necessary to obey Jewish laws when one chooses to follow Jesus. What habits or traditions do you expect others to obey in order to "be" Christians? Are such traditional expectations compatible with grace?

> How do God's grace and our faith work together to equal salvation?

Something that should be easy—that requires no work on our part—is a hard concept in this merit-oriented world. It was an even harder concept for the first-century Jews, who had lived their lives under the law. In his letter to the Jewish Christians living in Rome, Paul explained that grace had now replaced the law and that grace was available to everyone:

> But now the righteousness of God apart from the law is revealed, . . . through [our] faith in Jesus Christ, to all and on all who believe. For there is no difference [between Jews and Gentiles]; for all have sinned and fall short of the glory of God, being justified freely by His grace through the redemption that is in Christ Jesus, whom God set forth as a propitiation by His blood, through [His] faith, to demonstrate His righteousness, because in His forbearance God had passed over the sins that were previously committed, to demonstrate at the present time His righteousness . . . (Romans 3:21–26)

> Why is the law no longer necessary to experience God's grace? How does the abolition of the law work with the traditions many Christians follow today?

> Have you ever allowed nonbiblical ideas to interfere in your relationships with other Christians? What was the result of the disagreement? Was God honored by the way you treated your brother or sister in Christ?

> When faced with a conflicting opinion, how do you respond? Are you patient and willing to listen to the other person, or do you attack him, condemning his beliefs before understanding his point of view?

Realizing that our habits and traditions are unnecessary or incorrect is difficult. The first-century Jews were used to eating kosher food, but Paul and other apostles were telling them that what they ate no longer impacted their salvation. Grace had made all their laws obsolete. Even Peter, who was with Jesus throughout Jesus' three years of ministry, needed a supernatural vision to convince him to change his ways:

> Then he became very hungry and wanted to eat; but while they made ready, he fell into a trance and saw heaven opened and an object like a great sheet bound at the four corners, descending to him and let down to the earth. In it were all kinds of four-footed animals of the earth, wild beasts, creeping things, and birds of the air. And a voice came to him, "Rise, Peter; kill and eat."

But Peter said, "Not so, Lord! For I have never eaten anything common or unclean."

And a voice spoke to him again the second time, "What God has cleansed you must not call common." (Acts 10:10–15)

With Jesus' death, the merit system ended and grace was extended. The Jews didn't have to spend their lives meticulously following 613 laws, and the new Gentile Jesus followers didn't have to learn and then follow those same laws. Through one final sacrifice, the death of God's Son on the cross, all necessary sacrifices were completed for all people for all time. All debts were paid.

> Think of the last time you were offered something, maybe a job transfer or promotion, which had the potential to influence your life positively. Did you accept that gift, or did you reject it because "old habits die hard"? How did that gift change your life, or how do you think it would have changed your life had you accepted?

Discuss Grace

At the beginning of the session with your small group, watch Max's video that accompanies this Bible study. Take some time to discuss what you and your group members learned from chapter 4 in *Grace*, your personal studies of this week's lesson, and Max's message. Then consider these questions as a small group:

> Have you ever felt like there are certain things you need to do in order to be a Christian? What are these things?

> Have you ever been around someone who claims to be a better Christian than you are? What things did that person say you were wrong about? How did you respond?

> When was the last time you were offered something for free? Maybe you won a drawing or were given an extravagant gift. How did that make you feel? Could you accept it graciously, or did you feel the need to somehow repay the giver?

Conclusion / Prayer

Close your group time by taking prayer requests and praying for one another.

Notes

ACCEPTING THE GIFT OF WET FEET

Study Grace

Read chapter 5 from *Grace* before beginning your study this week.

In the last session, Max explained that grace is a free gift, something we can't earn through doing good deeds or by being good people. All we are asked to do is have faith that Jesus' sacrifice was enough to reconcile us to God, and through God's grace our sins are covered. No strings attached. But remember that grace is also an action. Once we have been covered by grace, the Holy Spirit compels us to show that grace to others.

We all know the Golden Rule: "Do unto others as you would have them do unto you" (Matthew 7:12; Luke 6:31). Jesus wasn't just a big talker; he practiced what he preached. The night before he was arrested, Jesus showed grace to Judas, the man he knew would betray him to his death. Jesus took the pose of a servant by removing his clothes, wrapping himself in a towel, getting down on his hands and knees, and washing the dirtiest parts of Judas and the rest of his disciples. Then he said,

"You are not all clean."

So when He had washed their feet, taken His garments, and sat down again, He said to them, "Do you know what I have done to you? You call Me Teacher and Lord, and you say well, for so I am. If I then, your Lord and Teacher, have washed your feet, you also ought to wash one another's feet. For I have given you an example, that you should do as I have done to you. (John 13:11–15)

If Jesus can show grace to a man complicit in his death, shouldn't we be able to offer grace to those around us? None of us have experienced the kind of pain that Jesus did as he hung on the cross, yet we allow just the memories of our emotional boo-boos to keep us from forgiving others. We hold grudges about everything, big and small, from wrecked cars to stomped-on tulips. We want to justify our stubbornness, saying forgiveness would be tantamount to approval, but it is not. Gracing your neighbor with forgiveness by replanting the tulip yourself and maybe giving her a bulb, too, does not give her license to mow down anything in your garden. That show of grace will actually give you an opportunity to build a relationship with your neighbor, and maybe remind her of your property lines. Likewise God does not approve of any sin; he graces us with forgiveness as he reminds us of his law, and the interaction brings us closer to him.

> Describe the first conversation you had with an antagonist after you were hurt. Were you able to explain your feelings without hurting the other person in return? Did you offer kindness and forgiveness, or were you still holding a grudge?

> If you offer a kind word to someone who has hurt you in the past, what do you think his or her response would be?

While Jesus was down on the floor wearing nothing but a loin cloth and washing his disciples' feet, the men must have felt awkward. They may have disliked feet as much as Max does. According to Scripture, no one dared to speak during this strange event—that is until Jesus reached Peter's feet. As usual, Peter spoke his mind:

"Lord, are You washing my feet?"

Jesus answered and said to him, "What I am doing you do not understand now, but you will know after this."

Peter said to Him, "You shall never wash my feet!"

Jesus answered him, "If I do not wash you, you have no part with Me."

Simon Peter said to Him, "Lord, not my feet only, but also my hands and my head!" (John 13:6–9)

When we are offered grace by others, it often looks strange, like a grown man getting down on the floor and washing your feet. Your first inclination is to reject it. You may wonder what the person will expect in return, because you've learned in life, "There's no such thing as a free lunch," so the saying goes. But genuine grace is free. Once Peter better understood what Jesus was doing, he got over his awkward feelings and wanted literally to bathe in grace.

> Think of a time when you've been offered grace. Did you reject it as strange or eagerly accept it?

> What was your response to the person who offered you that grace? Were you eager to reciprocate, or could you rest in the grace you received? Remember, no disciple got down and washed Jesus' feet when he had finished.

Paul reminded the Ephesians, "And be kind to one another, tenderhearted, forgiving one another, even as God in Christ forgave you" (4:32). Once we've accepted God's grace, he expects us to give it to those around us. It doesn't matter if we've been hurt. We should follow Jesus' example and Paul's reminder to "see to it that no one misses the grace of God and that no bitter root grows up to cause trouble and defile many" (Hebrews 12:15 NIV).

> Discuss an opportunity you've had to show grace to someone who wronged you in the past. Did you do it? What were the consequences?

> In what tangible ways can you show someone who has hurt you in the past that you are giving him or her grace now?

Discuss Grace

At the beginning of the session with your small group, watch Max's video that accompanies this Bible study. Take some time to discuss what you and your group members learned from chapter 5 in *Grace*, your personal studies of this week's lesson, and Max's message. Then consider these questions as a small group:

> Jesus was willing to touch the filthiest parts of his friends and his enemies. Have you ever shown grace to "unsavory" members of society?

> Consider the story Max told us about Victoria Ruvolo. What would have been your response to such a permanently disfiguring crime against you? Could you allow grace to free your attacker from guilt and free you from anger?

Conclusion / Prayer

Close your group time by taking prayer requests and praying for one another.

Notes

Grace is everything Jesus. Grace lives because he does, works because he works, and matters because he matters.

COMING CLEAN
WITHIN GRACE THAT ABOUNDS

Study Grace

Read chapter 7 from *Grace* before beginning your study this week.

All of us have secret temptations that threaten to separate us from God and from his people. In this session, Max confesses to us that one of his temptations is beer. As a pastor, he decided shortly after seminary that alcohol consumption probably wasn't compatible with ministry, so he wouldn't drink. But one hot Texas summer, he found himself hiding in his car with a beer in his hand. Max realized he was sinning, not because he was drinking a beer but because he was hiding it. He'd become a hypocrite.

Max is certainly not the first religious leader to fall to temptation. The greatest king of Israel, the man responsible for bringing God's presence into Jerusalem (2 Samuel 6), dedicated a season of his life to making stupid, idiotic, godless decisions. King David, in one short year, lusted after a married woman, committed adultery with her, lied to her husband, and had her husband killed. And then acted as if he'd done nothing wrong (2 Samuel 11). He was a hypocrite. However, David could not escape the guilt:

> When I kept silent, my bones grew old
> Through my groaning all the day long.
> For day and night Your hand was heavy upon me;
> My vitality was turned into the drought of summer.
>   (Psalm 32:3–4)

> David's guilt made him feel old, achy, and withered. How does guilt impact you? Do you have a physical response to the stress?

> How do those feelings of stress impact the way you relate to others? To God?

Only after the prophet Nathan confronted David with his sins in open court did David come clean with God (2 Samuel 12). His secret sin was no secret at all. Finally, he prayed,

Have mercy upon me, O God,
According to Your lovingkindness;
According to the multitude of Your tender mercies,
Blot out my transgressions.
Wash me thoroughly from my iniquity,
And cleanse me from my sin.
For I acknowledge my transgressions,
And my sin is always before me.
Against You, You only, have I sinned,
And done this evil in Your sight—
That You may be found just when You speak,
And blameless when You judge. (Psalm 51:1–4)

Hypocrisy, hiding your sins from others and thinking you are hiding them from God, is a rejection of the grace God so freely offers you. As the apostle John said, "If we say that we have no sin, we deceive ourselves, and the truth is not in us. If we confess our sins, He is faithful and just to forgive us our sins and to cleanse us from all unrighteousness" (1 John 1:8–9).

> When was the last time you confessed? It may have been in the form of an apology to a person you hurt, or it may have been an admission of your personal sins to God. What was the result of your honesty?

Not only does God want us to confess our sins to him, but he wants us to confess to each other. The apostle James, when writing to a church plagued with illness, said, "Confess your sins *to one another*, and pray for one another so that you may be healed" (James 5:16 NASB). As David learned, guilt and sin can have physical effects. Confess, and allow God not only to cleanse your soul but also to heal your body from the rigors of stress. Pray for others who are plagued with sin, and God will heal your relationships.

> Think of a time when someone confessed guilt to you. Were you quick with kind words, or were you quick with condemnation?

Yes, sin is a disease, an epidemic really. But confession is contagious too. Consider the experience of some exorcists in Ephesus. They did not follow Jesus, but they attempted to use his and Paul's name as part of an incantation to remove a demon from a man. The result? The demon confessed to Jesus' power and then made a mockery of the exorcists.

This became known both to all Jews and Greeks dwelling in Ephesus; and fear fell on them all, and the name of the Lord Jesus was magnified. And many who had believed came confessing and telling their deeds. Also, many of those who had practiced magic brought their books together and burned them in the sight of all. And they counted up the value of them, and it totaled fifty thousand pieces of silver. So the word of the Lord grew mightily and prevailed. (Acts 19:17–20)

God used the confession of a demon to incite the cleansing of the Ephesians who were blending their belief in Jesus with other pagan rituals. These people confessed their sins of following other gods, demonstrated their trust in God's grace by destroying cultic objects, and accepted his grace even in the shadow of the temple to the Greek goddess Artemis.

> As the exorcists demonstrated, words can have a powerful effect, even when the speaker is not fully aware of that power. Have you ever been impacted by someone's words or actions in spite of their intentions?

> Knowing that God can use any situation to ensure "the name of the Lord Jesus [is] magnified," are you more willing to confess your sins?

> How might your public confession affect others who have also sinned?

Discuss Grace

At the beginning of the session with your small group, watch Max's video that accompanies this Bible study. Take some time to discuss what you and your group members learned from chapter 7 in *Grace*, your personal studies of this week's lesson, and Max's message. Then consider these questions as a small group:

> What should you do when you've had a disagreement with a coworker?

> How should you respond to an apology? Can you offer that person grace, regardless of how big or how small his or her mistake was?

> Is there something you need to confess to God right now? Is this something you should share with the members of your small group?

Conclusion / Prayer

Close your group time by taking prayer requests and praying for one another.

Notes

CHOSEN
TO A **GUARANTEED**
PLACE IN THE **FAMILY**

Study Grace

Read chapter 10 from *Grace* before beginning your study this week.

Family is one of the most important structures in the Bible. God's first command to humanity was to "be fruitful and multiply" (Genesis 1:28). He wants us to have children and raise families. He later gave laws regarding the formation of families, further impressing his interest in them. The Old Testament told God's people whom they could and couldn't marry (Leviticus 18), what the penalties were for adultery (Deuteronomy 22:13–30), and how inheritances were to be divided among the children (Deuteronomy 21:17; Numbers 27:1–11). There were even safety measures built into the law, such as the Levirate Marriage, which protected the wife, the children, and any property owned by the dead man from harm by keeping it all in his name (Deuteronomy 25:5–6).

But what happened if both a man and his wife died, leaving under-age children? There were no rules for that.

Strangely silent from the law were rules about adoption, but adoption itself is a prevalent concept in the Bible. One of the most famous stories is that of Esther. There's a whole book devoted to her and how she kept the Jews safe during their Persian exile. None of her work would have been possible if she hadn't been adopted by her cousin, Mordecai.

Of course, the relationship between the adopter and the adoptee is not always so rosy. An adopted child may not always follow the path his or her parent desires. Just ask the greatest adoptive parent of all, God. In Romans 9:4, Paul told us that the people of Israel were God's adopted children. The Israelites, as Abraham's blessed descendants came to be called, were not perfect children. They regularly disobeyed God's commands, and he regularly had to punish them. (See basically the entire Old Testament for examples of this.) But no matter how bad his children were or how angry he got at them, God was their Father. In fact, he's still their Father today.

Paul told the Ephesian Jews and the Gentiles,

> Blessed be the God and Father of our Lord Jesus Christ, who has blessed us with every spiritual blessing in the heavenly places in Christ, just as He chose us in Him before the foundation of the world, that we should be holy and without blame before Him in love, having predestined us to adoption as sons by Jesus Christ to Himself, according to the good pleasure of His will. (Ephesians 1:3–5)

> God knew "before the foundation of the world" that he would make a way for all humanity to be reconciled to him. He knew sin would enter the world, and he knew grace would be necessary to overcome it. Are you willing to bestow grace to others, even if they don't see a need for it?

> Paul said we become God's children "by Jesus Christ." What did Jesus, now our Brother, do to enable us to be adopted by God?

Since Jesus died on the cross to reconcile everyone to God, everyone has the opportunity to become God's child. Adoption into his family is so much simpler than adoption into a modern family. There are no contracts, no lawyers, and no money changing hands. There are no waiting periods or household evaluations. Adoption only requires you to say *yes* to grace.

In his letter to the Romans, Paul tried to convince the mostly Jewish Jesus followers of the permanence of grace by comparing their acceptance of Jesus' sacrifice to a child's adoption into a family:

> For as many as are led by the Spirit of God, these are sons of God. For you did not receive the spirit of bondage again to fear, but you received the Spirit of adoption by whom we cry out, "Abba, Father." The Spirit Himself bears witness with our spirit that we are children of God, and if children, then heirs—heirs of God and joint heirs with Christ, if indeed we suffer with Him, that we may also be glorified together. (8:14–17)

In Rome, when a child was adopted, he lost all of his ties to his blood relatives. He became 100 percent a part of his new family, with full rights to inheritance. No difference was made between the adopted child and the natural child. That's the way it is for us and God. He loves us as much as he does his Son, and we are guaranteed the same inheritance that he has. Rest in the knowledge that God's grace has made you his child and that you are in no danger of being abandoned to your old relatives, sin and death.

Discuss Grace

At the beginning of the session with your small group, watch Max's video that accompanies this Bible study. Take some time to discuss what you and your group members learned from chapter 10 in *Grace*, your personal studies of this week's lesson, and Max's message. Then consider these questions as a small group:

> There are people in this world who are truly alone. Family members have died, and maybe friends are few. What could you say to introduce them to God's family? What could you do to show them God's love for all his children?

> Think of a difficult situation you've experienced. Had you accepted God's grace at that time? Could you feel his presence as you conquered the situation? By the grace of God, what did you learn from that period in your life?

Conclusion / Prayer

Close your group time by taking prayer requests and praying for one another.

Notes

To be saved by grace
is to be saved by
him—not by an idea,
doctrine, creed, or
church membership, but
by Jesus himself, who
will sweep into heaven
anyone who so much
as gives him the nod.

SUSTAINING AND SUFFICIENT GRACE

Study Grace

Read chapter 8 from *Grace* before beginning your study this week.

In the last six sessions, Max has taught us about the importance of God's saving grace. It is only through the grace he offers as a result of Jesus' sacrifice for our sins that we can live in the knowledge that we are saved. Once we are confident in that grace, we are encouraged to pass it along, to show it to others who need God in their lives.

But there is another kind of grace: a sustaining, sufficient grace. Once we are members of God's family, God is always with us. Consider Paul. In his second letter to the Corinthians, he mentioned that he suffered from "a thorn in the flesh" (v. 7). He wasn't specific; this "thorn" may have been a chronic disease, a physical disability, or maybe a persistent temptation to sin. He told his readers,

Lest I should be exalted above measure by the abundance of the revelations, a thorn in the flesh was given to me, a messenger of Satan to buffet me, lest I be exalted above measure. Concerning this thing I pleaded with the Lord three times that it might depart from me. And He said to me, "My grace is sufficient for you, for My strength is made perfect in weakness." Therefore most gladly I will rather boast in my infirmities, that the power of Christ may rest upon me. Therefore I take pleasure in infirmities, in reproaches, in needs, in persecutions, in distresses, for Christ's sake. For when I am weak, then I am strong. (2 Corinthians 12:7–10)

Paul, a man so blessed in intellect and spirituality, could have turned from God and trusted only in his own abilities. To keep this from happening, God *gave* him this thorn. But more importantly, God gave Paul the grace he needed to survive the struggle. God never permits a challenge without providing us the grace we need to meet it.

> In what way was Paul's thorn itself a demonstration of God's grace?

> When Paul asked God to remove the thorn, why do you think his request was denied? What does the perpetuation of Paul's pain allow God to do for him? For others?

> Why did Paul say he took "pleasure in infirmities, in reproaches, in needs, in persecutions, in distresses"?

> What did Paul mean by "when I am weak, then I am strong"?

The apostle John explained the constancy and abundance of God's grace as he introduced Christ to the world in his gospel account. In chapter 1 of John's gospel, we read that "the Word" was with God before the world was created and that "the Word" transformed into a human and lived on earth (v. 1). While Jesus was here, John and the other disciples saw his glory, just as Moses and the Hebrews saw God's glory before them in the Sinai desert. The same glory that represented God's covenant of grace to the Hebrews now represented God's new covenant of grace for all people:

> And the Word became flesh and dwelt among us, and we beheld
> His glory, the glory as of the only begotten of the Father, full
> of grace and truth. . . . And of His fullness we have all received,
> and grace for grace. For the law was given through Moses, but
> grace and truth came through Jesus Christ. (John 1:14, 16–17)

By one action—sending his Son—God multiplied exponentially the amount of saving grace needed by humanity and, at the same time, the amount of sustaining grace provided to them. Grace was now available to everyone on earth, not just the Jews, because grace was incarnate in Jesus, not in the law.

> How does Jesus' glory compare to God's glory in the Exodus story?

> How does Jesus' grace differ from the grace previously offered only by the law?

God didn't offer adoption to the world without providing enough grace to cover everyone. And he didn't sacrifice his only Son for only a few people to experience grace. It was for everyone. Paul reminded the Roman Christians, who were suffering

85

persecution and looking forward to the Second Coming, that all people (Jews and Gentiles) "whom He called, these He also justified; and whom He justified, these He also glorified. What then shall we say to these things? If God is for us, who can be against us? He who did not spare His own Son, but delivered Him up for us all, how shall He not with Him also freely give us all things?" (Romans 8:30–32).

Rely on God for your daily needs, rather than on yourself. If he is willing to grace your life with the big things—like saving your soul—then he can sufficiently sustain your life here on earth. Sustenance is a form of grace, even when we would rather be moving forward or doing something different. God's grace may not always appear in a form that we'd like, but it is always there when we need it. We should accept it and be grateful.

> Do you rely on God's grace for everything, or do you rely on yourself for some things? Is your self-reliance causing you to reject God's offer of grace in your life? How do you feel when you provide something for yourself as opposed to when you receive it as God's grace?

> When have you taken God's grace for granted? How could you have responded to his sufficiency and sustenance at the time?

> As you go through your day, be aware of moments of God's grace and write them down. What little things have you never noticed him gracing you with in the past? How would your day be different if he weren't supplying even your smallest needs?

Discuss Grace

At the beginning of the session with your small group, watch Max's video that accompanies this Bible study. Take some time to discuss what you and your group members learned from chapter 8 in *Grace*, your personal studies of this week's lesson, and Max's message. Then consider these questions as a small group:

> How has God shown his grace to you today? Can you see his presence in the things you do regularly?

> Think of a time when you doubted your ability to accomplish something. Did God show up and help you? What form did his grace take?

> In this debt-drowning society, what can you do to meet the needs of a family in your community who is struggling to keep food on their table? How does this activity look like the sustaining, sufficient grace God has given to you?

Conclusion / Prayer

Close your group time by taking prayer requests and praying for one another.

Notes